Mingling Voices

SERIES EDITOR: MANIJEH MANNANI

Give us wholeness, for we are broken
But who are we asking, and why do we ask?

PHYLLIS WEBB

National in scope, *Mingling Voices* draws on the work of both new and established novelists, short story tellers, and poets. The series especially, but not exclusively, aims to promote authors who challenge traditions and cultural stereotypes. It is designed to reach a wide variety of readers, both generalists and specialists. *Mingling Voices* is also open to literary works that delineate the immigrant experience in Canada.

SERIES TITLES

Poems for a Small Park
By E. D. Blodgett

Dreamwork
By Jonathan Locke Hart

Dreamwork

JONATHAN LOCKE HART

DREAMWORK

AU PRESS

© 2010 JONATHAN LOCKE HART

Published by AU Press, Athabasca University
1200, 10011 – 109 Street Edmonton, AB T5J 3S8

Library and Archives Canada Cataloguing in Publication

Hart, Jonathan Locke, 1956–
    Dreamwork / Jonathan Locke Hart.

(Mingling voices, ISSN 1917–9405)
Poems.
Issued also in electronic format (978-1-897425-71-8).
ISBN 978-1-897425-70-1

    I. Title. II. Series: Mingling voices

PS8565.A6656D75 2010   C811'.6   C2009-907007-3

Book design by Natalie Olsen, kisscutdesign.com
Painting by Jean Jackman Hart.
Printed and bound in Canada by Marquis Book Printing.

A volume in the *Mingling Voices* series:
ISSN 1917–9405 (Print)
ISSN 1917–9413 (Online)

FOR MARY, JULIA, AND JAMES

Acknowledgements

Many thanks to Manijeh Mannani, Series Editor, for including this book in her wonderful series, and to her colleagues at Athabasca University Press: Walter Hildebrandt, Director, Erna Dominey, Senior Editor, Brenda Hennig, Administrator, and Natalie Olsen, Designer, for welcoming, nurturing, and bringing out this book in such an elegant form. My thanks also to the two anonymous readers for the Press.

Dreamwork began in Princeton, New Jersey on 16 May 2002, and continued there, on trips, and in Edmonton, Alberta and Cambridge, England. On one of those voyages, I went to Yale and visited one of my teachers, Thomas M. Greene, a fine reader of poetry who was very ill. I remember him warmly

here. Years before, he had talked to me about how
Yves Bonnefoy combined being a poet and a critic.

The book was completed on 17 October 2002.
After letting the volume sit for a long while (which
is my usual way of working), I revised the poems.

I would like to express my gratitude to colleagues,
staff, and students at Princeton University (2000–
2002), particularly those connected with the Canadian
Studies Program, the Department of History, the
Department of Comparative Literature, and the
hockey team; I wish to thank the President and Fellows
of Clare Hall, Cambridge; I want to express thanks
to students, staff, and colleagues at the University
of Alberta, where I began to teach in January 1984.
I am especially proud of students whom I tutored,
supervised, or taught at Toronto, Alberta, Trent,
Harvard, Cambridge, Princeton, Sorbonne Nouvelle,
and elsewhere for all their accomplishments in poetry,
literature, history, and other fields.

To all those who encouraged or translated my
poetry over the years, I give thanks. In this regard, I
remember Robertson Davies, Robert Finch, Timothy
Findley, and Douglas LePan and thank, among others,
Alfred Alcorn, Sally Alcorn, Maria Athanasopoulou,
Anne Barton, E. D. Blodgett, Di Brandt, John Buschek,

Mary Baine Campbell, Sean Caulfield, Susan Colberg, Patricia Demers, Brian Edwards, Seamus Heaney, Robert Kroetsch, Nicole Mallet, Glenn Rollans, Jüri Talvet, Gordon Teskey, Nadezda Vashkevich, Fred Wah, and Robert Wilson.

To friends and family, more thanks. Others have inspired me for a long time: George Edward Hart, my father, is still writing into his mid nineties, and a painting by Jean Jackman Hart, my mother, appears posthumously as part of the cover design and in the book. My brothers and sisters, Charles, Gwendolyn, Deborah, Alan, and Jennifer have all been involved in their lives and careers with theatre, books, libraries, music, painting, architecture, film, and television. I salute my most impractical of families in this and earlier generations of painters, photographers, composers, musicians, and actors, amateur and professional.

To my wife, Mary Marshall, and our twins, Julia and James, I give deepest thanks.

Some along the way have asked me why I write poetry, and I ask why not.

JONATHAN LOCKE HART

Summer 2009

Introduction

Dreamwork is a collection of poems that bravely embraces history—personal, family, generational, national, and transnational. It traverses distant times and places, visits with the present, and carries forward into time. With much sensitivity and with no bias, Hart pays homage to antiquity, the classical, the modern, and the postmodern. This collection is a journey through time, a meditation on ruins and change, a serious undermining of temporal "facts," and a subtle defamiliarization of what we refer to as "history." "Call this settling with the Indians," Hart writes, in Poem 11:

> They surrounded the marsh
> And in the hush of night
> Killed the guards, with stealth

> Crept in and lit the dwellings
> And shot woman and child
> As they ran out asleep

Philosophical observations on everyday and historical events and the engines behind them—such as human greed, thirst for power, war, tyranny, and the universal desire for justice and democracy—are the substance of many poems in this collection, and they speak to Hart's profound look at life and his unsentimental nostalgia for a reality that dwells in dreams. Hart succinctly draws the situation for us in the following lines from Poem 75:

> ...   Peace and stillness
>
> may be the image of our sleep
> but be the freehold of our peace.

The poems also tackle the nature of knowledge and the irrefutable bond between wisdom and imagination. Imagination crystallizes in poetry, which is to Hart the purest form of language just as mathematics is the purest form of science:

> There is a gap in my head the dentist found
> Not sure what it is, he took x-rays.

> One of my friends went to the dentist
> And died weeks later of what they discovered.
>
> Poets are animists and dream
> The   is between word and world....
> Poem 96

A similar relationship exists between reality and dreams as seen in the opening lines of Poem 51:

> The utopia of dreams denies
> A doggerel we take as lies
>
> A willow hangs over the stream
> And is not abstract green.

One can almost hear the lyric voice in these poems asking about the importance of dreams and the value of poetry. The speaker in Hart's poetry seems to ask, What is the point of having a head without a heart?

Unlike the narrators in Dante's *Divine Comedy*, and despite their literary merit, many other assuming works of the same nature, the persona in *Dreamwork* does not land on any celestial terrain in his quest to define wisdom. The only certainty the speaker in these poems seems to be aware of is the undeniable link that exists between imagination, dreams, poetry, and wisdom.

This certainty journeys to a metatextual level upon which the speaker—reminiscent of the poet's Romantic predecessors—is heard to ruminate on the figure of the poet and the nature of his vocation. Many years ago, Percy Bysshe Shelley called people's attention to the importance of poetry and deemed poets "the unacknowledged legislators of the world." Centuries later, echoing Shelley, Hart describes the life of a poem in a possible world where dreams have become words:

> Something futile: crafting
> A poem, translating a dream
>
> Into words. The possible world
> Takes hold
>
> In unseen roots.
> Poem 52

The probing into the nature of poetry culminates in Poem 73, where the speaker announces the inevitability of poetry in the face of those who would deny it:

This poem —like prose
verse —tense, terse, loose

A little like dreams
builds a logic

That despite
the rain will come.

Last but not least, I should note that despite its
dreamlike quality, *Dreamwork*, much like Hart's
previous poetry, is deeply rooted in landscape.
Place and time are equally important to Hart.
The juxtaposition of historic places with the more
recent and contemporary settings in this collec-
tion is in line with the continuity of thoughts that
have preoccupied man and woman then and now,
and they speak to the exuberance of the motifs in
these poems, which have been conceived mostly
on trains connecting cities in the northeastern
United States.

MANIJEH MANNANI
Edmonton, 2009

1.

Dreams lie at angles to the sun
The sweat is real, the possible worlds
Are not to some. Diviners have read

Their entrails. Freud
Crafted their guidebook, conjured them
On a hot summer's evening. Dreams

Embarrassing, enthralling, are
Our third selves
A third of ourselves: dreams

Deny, defy. The bog they pulled you from
Where you had plunged into the peat
Unconscious, thousands of years before

Pieced you together, mud and sand,
As evidence
A dark wound from the sun.

2.

Smoke and snow blow slowly
From pine to pine

The dream of peace rises like yeast
The wind erases footprints

A kiss is a trace
A whisper of exile.

3.

Dreamwork is the sum
Of sleep and waking.

The brush by the rail
Grows out of anything:

Wires and poles, bridges
And cable-boxes are not the keys

To sleep: they carry an invisible
World. Love is an unseen science.

4.

Why are you haunted, son, by the night
Wander the halls when the sun escapes

Fear the beyond as a mortal
And fall asleep spent?

You wrote poems at the root
Broke the spine of myth

Before you could write.
You are the signs

The incantations of sleep
Amid the roar of thunder.

5.

Gardens are more interesting than dreams
Roses smell better in gardens than in sleep

Oaks are welcome in some dreams.
Dreams are unacknowledged

And, being nothing,
Legislate nothing.

6.

The world is actuarial
I have always had trouble with death

The past is a table
Until we look at it

Dead brilliance in the night sky
Traces of something — the memory of you.

7.

The heat of sheets
The play of type

When the ink dries
Names will cool in the index.

8.

Readers die like poets
Death is not a dream

Commas are fardels
Quartos will have

Their fling. Devils rise
Above their inky cloak

A child cries on this train
Easy to hear, hard to read.

9.

The ephemera of my flesh
Touched yours, endured when
The sun

Rained through the forest
And the light licked your hair
And came to rest in mythology.

10.

All that is left

Is wisdom. The marshes at Westport
Have almost receded, the cars
Shimmer by the trees

The white of boats on the water, the rust
Of rails, all take time. The first
Glimpse — saplings sprout

By the bridge. A disconsolate woman
Talks to herself because her phone
Has cut out, just when the vast

Atlantic comes into view
Her office is ours: she tries again
My mind in search of dreams.

11.

They surrounded the marsh
And in the hush of night
Killed the guards, with stealth

Crept in and lit the dwellings
And shot woman and child
As they ran out asleep

Call this settling with the Indians.

12.

What
Made you hang those witches
Weigh testimony and not

What did your dreams say
Or were they the devil's work?
I am remembering that statue

Of my ancestor, Roger Conant,
And the graves of my forebears
Hathorne and White.

What could they have made
Of the place they fled to?
What tyrant king could do worse?

13.

Election
Why I chose the quiet life till now

At Salem
I studied irony or did it study me?

14.

The guilt of invasion and slavery
Even long after

Violence comes like a hammer

And we are caught, with bloody hand,
Crammed between nostalgia and utopia.

15.

The necks of dead witches
Snapped long ago

Bulging eyes, bruised skin
Muffled cries, kill the wind

Sold to the living
Perhaps in remembrance.

16.

The pain bites
The rain slaps.

                The crows
Sway in the wind

That turns leaves like memories.
Quiet you were, quiet you are
Choosing each word

                    like a pebble
The day overcast as you quote

Whitman here in New Haven
The ebullient poet who lifts

The frailty of flesh, lights
The mind with shimmering sound.

17.

The weariness of the marrow
Held in the deep cold of a prairie
The wires hiss
At the insouciance of mercury.

I could go there in obscurity
The whisper of steel strung out
In the rumour of night.
The inhereness of winter

Encloses us
The child unsuspecting

He would be here now. On a train
Again, its rumble — sway on the bridge
Obliterating the music of the spheres
The syncopated silver water dancing.

18.

The commuter lot lies vacant: the markets
Have gone south like geese. So much for

The long summer of childhood: the gravel bed
Is barely visible, the Atlantic peering over

The spring brush. Trade feeds us and fleets
Like the evanescence of words: how do we endure

And turn with the seasons and make a sound
Between and beyond cry of birth, moan of death?

19.

Meditations
On justice as we move through Rye
Derailed by nightmare.

They plant
A field against war: the gaunt child
Haunts the orchard. The epidemic

Closes the theatre.

20.

The light on the platform
At New Rochelle is not so obvious:
The surface refracts, reflects, absorbs
A man on the train repeats the word "sports"

Like a chant. I have ears that remember
Conversations years ago: the houses on
Leafy streets beyond Pelham Station
Are yoga to incantation. Cross purposes

Are not like tacking in a strong wind.
Sleep without rest exhausts, annoys
And makes no buffer against accident
And aggression. The streetlights are on before dark.

21.

Too much history and not enough time:

As we move through the apartment blocks
Towards Grand Central Station, small moments

Matter most — traces long after.

22.

We begin in a tunnel: when we emerge
Manhattan is at our backs, and we
Plough across the Hudson manifest

And industrial and technical rhythms
Play on ear and eye.

We come up to the slate slab
Of clouds, the sun slicing between them.
The green trees are luminescent
Lungs thrilling—spring evening

The air brushes the grasses, the iron
Scaffolding, four generator stacks, electric
Grid extends to the left, and we head west.

23.

The distance from New Haven to Princeton
Is more than a metaphor. The scar
In Manhattan is hard to imagine
The people remarkably calm.

Dreams pass through New York — open port,
Cross-roads, marketplace, pool of capital
Clichés chasing a dynamic trace.
A wound lies on the brow, the smoke and blood

Have cleared and gone underground. Some weep
At night; others drift, confess, deny
Against the imminent night sky. What will
Seep into the marrow? The distance from

Princeton to New Haven finds no harbour.
The ghosts can do nothing to heal
The unsleeping horror of terror and violence.

24.

'Listen carefully,' a poster commands
Rope, wire, rail line the platform
At Linden.

A man without a ticket, drunk, proclaims
Something as if from the Book of Job.

Two girls break into song. They're on for one stop.

The train is its own engine of meaning —
It moves in the dusk like a sliver.

25.

Someone conducts a deal
On the train

Perhaps he is thinking
Of a hummingbird.

26.

Reality is hard to corner
That's a fact: the sycamore
Is not a myth.

This is the time
Of day when the windows on the train
Meld the dark shadows of trees with the faces

Of the passengers.

27.

He built a house
and found that brick
straw, mud would not do

That no matter how strong
the matter against wind
rain, sun, it could not

Withstand what humans
could do to it. Neither
could the river erode

The ruins that were left.
What is ill leaves a trace
In the complaint against carpenters.

28.

What hedges do is hard to tell.
Some are listed in the Doomsday Book.

Hedges are about lives
Not quite in view.

He cut his hand on electric hedge clippers
His flesh

Not rose petals. Hedges are themselves
Scars, metaphors, a wistfulness
For Eden, nostalgia, a backing

Into the future. We might hedge
Our bets with reveries and work
On land and time like a green river.

29.

At Edison Station I remember

Scars like the rails we ride. Edison
made a promise against the ebb
of energy in the shadow of the guns.

30.

Civility is a dream
receding

as the train pulls away.
There was a time

before trains, perhaps
before metaphors. The day

is still, the sun rides
the clouds, the luminescent

green of bud and leaf
seeks the shade of peace.

31.

Lilac and sun
roll by the window

Of the subway train.
The glass

Seals off the scent.
Remembrance returns

That exhibit of forgotten
lives, those Mohawk doctors

Those preachers on the underground
railroad, the Canada of their mind.

32.

How history forgot that a Black woman
wrote the song Canadian troops marched to
in the Great War, that an Iroquois leader

Could have a state funeral in 1907
in Toronto, having been a doctor
and the leader of the International

Foresters. How history forgot forgetting
how Joseph Brant helped Canada
to exist, the Native names of these great

Sachems on both sides of the border.
How history forgot Moctezuma's own words
despite the broken spears, voices of the vanquished

How the Indios were driven into the mountains
As if passive constructions could allay
How history forgot who did what to whom.

33.

How I forgot that my soapbox was broken
How it had had its ribs kicked in

As if the smell of blood were on our hands
how I forgot all this and more. Stanzas

Cannot hold the world, contain the day.
The machines grind up the asphalt

And lay down a new surface, as if a road
Were more than a metaphor.

How I forgot that choruses
Are not always about herds.

Hector could not hector Troy
Even after Helen hellenized it
And the horse had kicked over my milking stool.

34.

Could the worm
eat a human heart

even in heroic times
when the gods spoke poetry?

Everything
can be taken out of context

a weariness descends, and gardens
although eaten up, take on

more than meaning can bear, like
a certain nostalgia for meaning.

35.

Some day I will write an elegy to Roger Conant
Say that he begot

A town
Caught between election and hysteria

The blue of the Atlantic extending
Between home and exile. Some day I will

Write an elegy, ask questions
About witches and scapegoats

Note that he wasn't there that year.
Some day I will

Try to do something a little different
And leave him to his own dignity and silence.

36.

The crushed rock mounts against the chain-link fence
The coils of barbed wire line the top rung.

After the camps, this wire by the rail in Newark
And on the brick fences in the colleges in Cambridge

Form lines that the Elizabethans might have misread.
Even pastorals are subject to history.

I dream with stones in my shoes.

37.

The winter of our breath
Hung in our marrow

The frost of your lips
Nipped like memory

The leaves did not

Know what country they were in
The dust fell like snow on your hair.

38.

What gift there was
You would not say

Why the day was like
Night no one would advise

How the wind came up
Silence would not own

Where they had been
No one could tell

Who brought this out
When all was done?

39.

I could not choose the choice lyric
The dreamtongue of a dreamscape

Puns like eyelids, tears
Tearing my heart apart. This kind

Of dream I fear for its rhetoric. I look
Out at the platform at Jersey Avenue.

40.

Perilous these night terrors
That hand grabs my throat

The mind beads and quivers
Context flees like a defeated
Army: the cloud a mushroom

That came over and over
Since I was a child.

41.

There are flags in the forest
That flap and hang
Old Glory

Fingerprints in the wood.

                              Tenets
Are not roses.

The nature of a republic
Is not the republic of nature?

42.

You both see something in the world
I cannot.

One day you came stereo into the world,
One sleepy as if awakened
The other wired, wide-eyed

All limbs pushing the air like a question.

The Mediterranean was clear

And the epistemology of the sun
Blinded us all before we headed back to the snow.

43.

In this lifeworld
we reinvent our bones

Begetting worlds

The lake shaking

We are buried under
that tree by the swing.

44.

Lamentation of the ur-world
A red wagon empty rolls past

She is not liminal or nominal
But has on a delicate dress

Her hands are broken with words
But her eyes stay the road.

45.

'Remember me,' he said
Dead in the garden.

'Why are there threads?'
She asked,

Having drowned in a stream
The symbology of flowers

Up to her neck. The exegesis
Of mothers

Perplexed me as poetry vanished
Lips and wounds

Grew as wide as the red door
All bodies and silence.

46.

Not even Narcissus
Can find a definite reflection

He spoke
Of doxa and anti-doxa

But soon forgot that in the sun
That beat and melted all before it.

The fish were not interested
In gnomic indeterminacy

And the sweat poured from his head
Like a curtain and stung his eyes.

47.

Life is long, lives are short
The heat of the day will stick

In my marrow like memory:
The t-shirt clings to my collar bone

Like fingers to a raft. She is
Ineffable, her lips an opening

To a world. The Atlantic
Pounded beyond these metaphors

Like stones. For a while even the waves
Were stones. Her eyes were the sky

And there was an end to it: I buried
Myself in her embrace but was not

Dead. The earth loved its seasons best
Its flowers wrists and eyebrows.

48.

No authority resides
In the wisdom of the tides

No wisdom can hide
In a place where time has hid

Nonsense is not no sense
Logic is not the logos

Or all of it. When we were
Young we did not care

For off-rhymes and small
Green raspberries that fell

By the tracks. Philosophy was
Difficult for the bliss

Of the hummingbird hovering above
The nectar, and we would dive

Without looking past
A lake dark as glass.

49.

Stranded, the forest of night
Tangled, subjunctive, my toes white

Roses burning, night panic
Shake me, mimics

Death. Music can be cruel
Strung out of school

Numbers chasing grace
The place of poetry in plague time.

50.

The sun made your flesh
Russet, your eyes through mesh

Peering out, and in the haze
Ariadne lost in the maze

The invisible world has fled
The realm of Arthur's bed

Archimedes and Galen had no clue
About the chemistry of the morning dew.

51.

The utopia of dreams denies
A doggerel we take as lies

A willow hangs over the stream
And is not abstract green.

Do we see the same tree and wall
As those we pass by the Raritan Canal?

52.

Something futile: crafting
A poem, translating a dream

Into words. The possible world
Takes hold

In unseen roots. A wood may be
One organism.

The birch on the point
Is suspended, its roots exposed as the lake
Eats the loam, the sun dancing on its leaves

The wind
Drops, the ink is fire.

53.

He moves again
As the summer fades, as if philosophy
Could guard against the ruin of time.

The wind howls over
The sea.

The edge
Of the moon on the mountain gives
Temporary solace.

Our blindness cannot

Track our somnambulation. The road lies
Broken, nostalgia like sails on and over
The horizon. Buried touch. Moved he moves.

54.

The frost on the window
Is ice on the lake

This at midnight might now
Resolve like a dew and end there

The death of noise and smoke
In the hurry of words.

55.

He saw the grass bend
In the wind, the blood

Not eupeptic. That night
Might fall for ever

Before flesh came with the rain
And destiny, like reason,

Had splintered.

56.

You are a refugee
The corporate army trudging
Nature rolling back

Exhaust, exhaustion
For

57.

The elms on a cloudy night
Are indifferent to argument

A life that asks too many questions
Is like one that asks too few

A nightmare. Rain in the dust
Vanishes in the night.

How do we swim in mountain lakes
Without armies of the night in pursuit?

58.

The prose of love
Will not live

Will stutter, words
Loose and absurd.

59.

Bury me in the boneyard of the stars
These words traces in the way

The world came to be.
This tongue a lost fossil

Earth
Receive these dreams, stardust remains.

60.

The hedges on Herschel Road
Spill over on to the pavement

Pollen wafts from the purple garden
As if the translunar world were

An afterthought. Places have
A personal haunting: as I look

Across St John's field from Grange Road
Embers die in the night of stars, though it is

Day still. Glades may seem quaint
But they are all we have for now.

61.

I would write a homage to Henry Adams
A tenant farmer who left the West Country

For New England, an ancestor who begot
John, John Quincy, Henry and many of us

More obscure, all tenants
Wrestling to throw off our own tenancy.

The Massachusetts of his mind
Was not of slavery and the plunder

Of King Philip's War. His garden
Was still a dream.

62.

The dream names of my ancestors
And the families they married or knew

Fade and are torn up like thousand-year
Hedges: Throckmorton, Churchill, Coggeshall

Their relation and voices hard to surmise
A little like Balboa displaced

Into poetry: remembrance

Of all the anonymous who made them up
Before the fashion of written history.

63.

The story of this earth might be
an Etruscan fable

Some chose
to avoid the brazen cauldrons

Or the eruptions of the unconscious
Enceladus. All I want to do

Is get through this wood
leaving all rumour for your love.

64.

She sought out the fire
the relics of him left

More and more
her blood, her fame

Were all consumed
abandoned except to verse

Far greater than lamentation
and the stillness of death

Nature unfolds.

65.

The ghost of her gaze
plays on me in the ruin

At Bury St Edmunds,
the sprawl of the grounds

The flowers are peacocks
by a deep green blanket

And the books of the abbey library
have long since been displaced

By change and barbarism. They cry
at the threshold, the remains

Of their days in an urn
the vale a mourning the dead

Cannot hear. The children gone
are given to time and its monsters

All too human but changed in myth
to make the nightmare almost bearable.

66.

In the quiet of this circle
between sun and thunder cloud

The martyr buried here
cries, whispers drowned out

The archeology of lost souls
and the almost simultaneity of it all

Perishes in the dream of the present
its future moves already past in a breath.

67.

The shadow of the shadow's face
Leaves the reflection of our grace
In shards where the mirror lies cracked
For all the flesh our souls lacked.

Making sense of what we did not make
Parsing what is life, dream, rack
We live on, sound and light long after
What began with hope or disaster.

68.

What is left is left in the gunyard
Ash shrouded

Their eyes. The taste of dust
Lay, quiet
Fell over the land, the wrist

Bled but could not break
Time.

Salt stung his eyes. Echoes
Of nothing like snow
Landed on what might have been.

69.

The floods came and technē failed
The earth caved in, the walls buckled
And people who never got carried away

Did. Never live by a river
Even though it feeds you in the sun.
The drought we knew, slivered

Moon over the arid earth, done
In the dry night sky, blue
With desire. Now the rivers run

Into a lake not of our making
And, waking, we fear what breath
We hang on, rue the pale and dead.

70.

The tanks watched, almost at war,
Bombs in mailboxes had blown, the stir
Of terror in the air, and we, in the car,

Moved on the way
And illusion had left a dew

Tinged with gunpowder. I recall
The photo of the high commissioner, ill
And gaunt, and flickering from the stale

Light the television image of the trunk
Where they had stuffed the dead minister.

My youth in these arpents, not sure
What the snow would bring on this far shore.

71.

The grit by the track
stuck in his shoes

He would dive to dig
clay pockets under
the deep clear of the water

Crab apples among the rhubarb
stung his guts

His dog plunging for a branch
long submerged, almost rotting
before he knew the ravages of time.

72.

These hedges teem. The blood
on the ground still stains

The grass without remains.
The bees suck the purple clover

At dusk. The mist is scarred
in the dream of night. The king's

Fictions persist.
                    Children

Play in the hedges, and lovers
dwell in their bowers, borders

That are and are not
in life and in art.

73.

This poem —like prose
verse —tense, terse, loose

A little like dreams
builds a logic

That despite
the rain will come.

The eruption
of people on this island means
most of us don't know where we will lie

How bones have been moved
from the village green to obscurity
ruining all continuity

The moon on the walk.

74.

These floods blew through the streets
and bore away people like pillars

of salt and almost tore their hearts
and stopped their mouths, as though

the rains would never cease, and no
break in the clouds would promise

relief.
          The wake and ebb

could hold no prediction. Ancient
chapels, paintings, frescoes, furniture

were borne away. Not even irony
could spare them, the dream of dry land.

75.

They that eat the land
leave nothing but scraps

for the dead, they that
spill the blood of ghosts

have small compassion
for the children the wars

have left, they that absolve
themselves for all they have done

and blame those who strike back
after all this time, excuse

tyranny and death, as if they were
wind in the grass. Peace and stillness

may be the image of our sleep
but be the freehold of our peace.

76.

These bones on the prairies are frozen
to the marrow: the riverbed riffles

with wind through the long brown grasses
the stubble from harvest toppled

by snow against the wire fences. The short days
weigh the soul like blanched straw

after baling. There have always
been those who collect rents

and waste the land, shrink
the summer, lace the blood

with a slow poison. Some lazy greed
gives no rest to the dreamless head.

77.

He considered his poems
secrets, as if caught
in some act too terrible

more shameful than sweat
on naked flesh, askance
in the garden embowered.

No one in his clan or town
wrote or read lines from nature
sublimated desire in the measure

of words. From the sea where he stood
his round face, bearded, his eyes
peering from horn-rims, he descanted

as though someone else, on love and death
and how that ate the theme of blood and bone
how he reached for something

beyond his nose, past the prose
and clatter of each day and the night
he feared and loved to the end.

78.

On the frontier poetry is a sign
something almost irrelevant, not quite
benign, a signatory to a contract

nearly broken that sweat and grease
and money matter most. How much
could he cheat books and theories

twilight and the rose would mean
success, cars and clothes, rhymes
of a different order, from paradigms

that take account of a different music.
He carved out his guilt and perverse
talent in chapbooks of uncertain design

and the smell of pulp and coal
were really no different than fumes
in gridlock by the exchange

in a town, now a vast conurbation,
his family left so long ago now
when the Revolution had them by the throat.

79.

How are theories like dreams?
Questions were like

hairs on the arms of the surgeon
before he went under

the Dutch painters painted
tables with fruit and fowl

this great table is more from a country kitchen
than one that Hippocrates might have owned.

80.

My son doesn't like to go to sleep
or wake up: he defers both moments
like a commuted sentence, picking up

a ball, chasing an enemy off the screen
pressing all the buttons, moving from room
to room, or, once asleep, not really wanting

to leave the world he seemed to dread
the night before. Dream, fancy, fantasy

imagination all ill-defined define
the shadows the sun chases across
his face. The shirt of night

slips into the rags of day, and he
manages to make those hours beyond
transition sing like the barn swallow.

81.

My daughter yearns for sleep
after a day brimming, she picks up
her blue blanket, her eyes weighted

with time, and tries to stay past
the moment that seems to erase
itself with a yawn. She pauses

moves past her twin, hawkish
with the night, and turns in
her reading still on her mind

for the rest, the deep dream
of a sleep of her own definition
until she bounds from bed

with the sun rising, a compass
to her breath and the paradox
that is the fulcrum of her grace.

82.

This dream knows no decency:
it embarrasses my waking self, serving
up all that sickens me about myself

and others, the sullied obfuscation
of the flesh, the concupiscence of the soul,
the confusion of the faculties. The mud

lies neck-deep, and the silence of terror
seeps long after the crimes. This dream
is what might be as if it were: the sweat

stains the sheets. What kills me by inches
is that as I walk now I almost know
that in these fields whatever the worst

I could imagine, asleep or awake,
could not measure beside what was
in the pathology of a time we call history.

83.

The tribe of sleep has broken in
the walls buckling
the winds shaking our bones

Cats call in the alleys, earthly
mansions burn, others lie in ruin
the young howl, the old sob

And the seven hills smoke
like a typology, beasts like icons
or an apocalypse burst

Into the heart of time and this city.
All that can be feared is, what was
civil falls to the cinder-hearts

Of the invaders. We who crouch
also conceal, we hide to save our hides
the barbarity within us.

The sun breaks on the quiet
of our childhood. Those stars were your eyes
in a hyperbole beyond commonplace.

84.

The myth of his tongue
the two portals of dream
keep his mask fast to his face

the cast of the sun, the spume
dancing across him, the gates
of horn and ivory on either side

as he returns from the war
the gorgeous illusions, perdurable truths
tugging at him, the image of her

before him. The homecoming
is always there between tears
and blood. His arrows would

no longer bleed invention
or fabrication — her eyes
burn in his brain, his fingers trembling.

85.

He searched in the lane
he overturned every
garden chair and stereotype

he pursued wishes with unbated breath
crossed the Xanadu of elemental flesh
the rush of lust not even able

to obscure the pedantry of the quest
no word in his tongue for Traumdeutung

amid her laughter, wasps on the peaches
digging deeper, better there than her bruised
flesh — the cauchemar of the dark wood.

86.

Rage against what time
the never that will not
the bounds that cannot

be redressed. Howl
as if eyes were

dead stars. The silence
now lies beyond the ear
yearn for peace.

87.

Not to turn
emerging from sleep

not quite sure what might be
that she might

turn to salt or cinder
her hair as if

it never were, the leaves afire
on hills too old for emotion

the orbit of consequences leaving
the fall back to as it were.

88.

'Freud was wrong,' he told me,
forgetting about Jung, and the sleep

that overcame Endymion never
came up again, but who was right
she thought, the twilight being
all or none. Theories have ghosts

that are poems. The lake was heavy with refuse, the
carelessness of souls
too callous or thoughtless to leave
the waters alone. Only a hundred years

before they drank from this body
now festering. 'Marx was wrong,' he
said, but who was right, she thought
and wondered whether profit needed

redefining. Images lie broken: the dumps
are ubiquitous, the rain burning their eyes.

89.

Dreamwork is an oxymoron
except when the sheets are wet
with the wrestle of night
when music

changes sharply. The pull of sun
and moon moves tides and blood
the uncertain wisdom of the unseen
and unremembered becomes something

unintended. The almost labour
of the nearly dead lies caught
in the net, a web in the diaphragm
between breath and naught. This

fable breaks up the prose of day
with the waste of poetry, the dance
of an alternative world, the blue
of her sleeve fluttering in the wind.

90.

The blue of this pen is almost a sky
Turns like a falcon over the field
Turns away from promises in clay

As if all were one and the dead
Alive with dreams to match. The loss
Of years are the blue of these eyes.

91.

The silence of these trees
A lake calm and dark

There is so
Much I cannot see while waking
With these eyes

So much eludes scrutiny
The light

And shadow sent along the nerves.
I have come back
To the stillness

The smoke the lightning
Spreads over the hill.

92.

Another burial, never the last,
Takes away. The dun earth

Receives its guest: as the moon
Wanes, the dew melts.

Words come and are undone
But stay for now, this sturdy dream.

93.

My great aunt sat at her window
The London sky beyond the heath
Alight with bombs, her mother,

A few years dead, had seen zeppelins
In the Great War. How the bomb-fires
Over Germany consumed young and old.

They died with ash in their mouths
The cinders smouldered after the bones
Could no longer laugh.

My grandfather, now dead, had left
For a place where
No bombs fell.

94.

The night sweats convey, confuse
Confound the sanity in a wrist of light
A tenuous angel-hair

The wind an anxious
Scapegoat. The city is besieged
The almost dead eat what they can

The scene from Brueghel before him.
No Gothic novel can devise the shame
He feels each night this visitation comes.

What time is
More barbarous than the present? Dream-tenses
Might shift.

In this dream-grammar, verbs tilt at
The impossibility of time, the drowned
Couple, like poets, dredged from the glacial lake.

95.

The elders are all dead
They have been stuffed away in wood

Or cast upon a pyre
Put out to sea wrapped in fur

As if they were warriors still
Or dropped in a moat from a castle wall

They store their dreams in vaults
Stir from the earth when the murder of time,

The people they had been with,
Have let them down.

The elders are grown stiff
And the wind has broken their staff.

96.

There is a gap in my head the dentist found
Not sure what it is, he took x-rays.

One of my friends went to the dentist
And died weeks later of what they discovered.

Poets are animists and dream
The   is between word and world.

Maps and films can be read
Even in the cavities of the head.

This gap I hope is no mortal abscess
The kind that makes for mortal rest.

97.

I have wandered many places
My memories fading, no Aeolian harp.

Has it come to this so long after?
I used to count railway ties

As I walked, kick stones between the rails.
The hummingbirds would hover over wild flowers

By the lake, where ancient rocks had erupted.
The smell of your hair is older than my knowledge.

98.

The beautiful ecstasy of words
is sand in my hand

The lovely dream of sound
is a turning in bed

The delicacy of a turn
returns in a vitality

Borne on the edge of water
inward, skyward, something

Beyond lips and fingers
a soul in an effigy

yearning for the real
dust a pollen on the tongue.

Index of First Lines

Note to reader: Numbers indicate poem numbers.

Jonathan Locke Hart has published poetry for over twenty-five years in literary journals such as *Cimarron Review*, *Grain*, *Harvard Review*, *Mattoid*, *Quarry*, and *The Antigonish Review*. Translations of his poems have been published in Estonian, French, Greek, and other languages. He has given readings in Australia, Canada, Estonia, France, Germany, Slovenia, the United Kingdom, the United States, and elsewhere. His recent volumes of poetry are *Breath and Dust* (2000), *Dream China* (2002), and *Dream Salvage* (2003). Professor Hart began teaching at the University of Alberta in 1984 and has also held visiting appointments at Cambridge, Harvard, Princeton, Sorbonne Nouvelle, Toronto, and Zaragosa.

Recycled
Supporting responsible use
of forest resources
www.fsc.org Cert no. SGS-COC-003153
© 1996 Forest Stewardship Council

Marquis imprimeur inc.

Québec, Canada
2010

This book has been printed on 100% post consumer
waste paper, certified Eco-logo and processed chlorine free.